Doyli
to the
Rescue

Saving Baby Monkeys
in the Amazon

Cathleen Burnham

CRICKHOLLOW BOOKS

Crickhollow Books is an imprint of Great Lakes Literary, based in Milwaukee, Wisconsin, an independent press publishing quality fiction and nonfiction.

Our titles are available from your favorite bookstore or from book-trade wholesalers or library jobbers. For a complete catalog of all our titles or to place educational bulk orders, visit our website:

www.CrickhollowBooks.com

For a teacher's guide & other resources for this WAKA series (World Association of Kids & Animals), which includes *Doyli to the Rescue* and other books about kids around the world involved in grassroots projects to protect endangered wild animals and their habitats, visit:

www.WAKABooks.org

Doyli to the Rescue: Saving Baby Monkeys in the Amazon
© 2015, Cathleen Burnham

Photos by Cathleen Burnham, with additional photography by Kenyon Burnham and Bay Burnham.
Book design by Melissa Thoroughgood.

ISBN: 978-1-933987-22-4

Note: this replaces an earlier softcover edition, ISBN 978-0-9836666-0-8, published by the author in 2011.

Summary: *Doyli to the Rescue: Saving Baby Monkeys in the Amazon,* by photodocumentary journalist Cathleen Burnham, is an inspiring real-life story of a 10-year-old girl named Doyli who rescues orphaned wild monkeys, then cares for them until they can be released back into their natural habitat in the Amazon rainforest.

BISAC Codes
JNF003010 JUVENILE NONFICTION / Animals / Monkeys
JNF003330 JUVENILE NONFICTION / Animals / Baby Animals
JNF003270 JUVENILE NONFICTION / Animals / Endangered
JNF038050 JUVENILE NONFICTION / People & Places / Caribbean & Latin America
JNF037020 JUVENILE NONFICTION / Science & Nature / Environmental Conservation & Protection

TOPICS: Amazon rainforest, global kids, youth activism, wild animal rescue & conservation.

First Crickhollow Books Edition

Printed in Canada

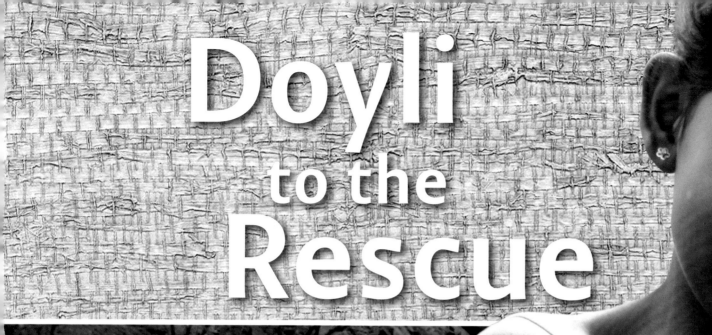

Doyli
to the
Rescue

Saving Baby Monkeys
in the Amazon

photos & text by

CATHLEEN BURNHAM

CRICKHOLLOW BOOKS

South America

North
Atlantic
Ocean

COLOMBIA

ECUADOR

Iquitos

Amazon River

PERU

BRAZIL

*Lima

BOLIVIA

South
Pacific
Ocean

South
Atlantic
Ocean

The Amazon

Bogotá

COLOMBIA

ECUADOR

Doyli's house

Napo River

Iquitos

PERU

Lima

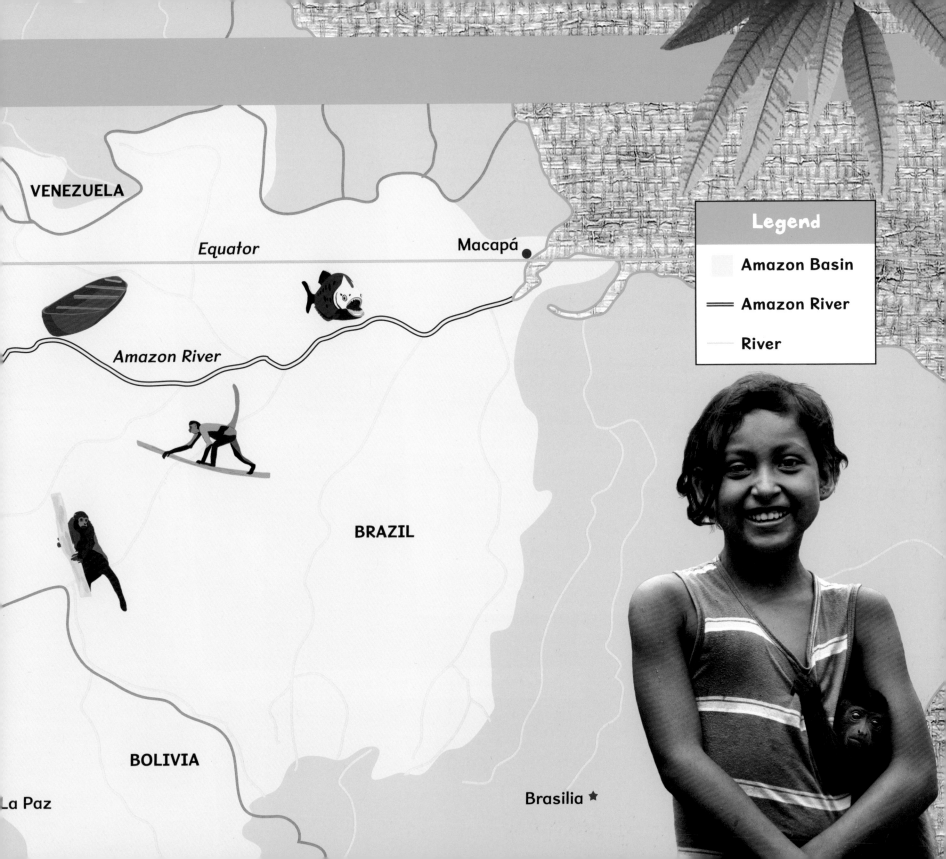

VENEZUELA

Equator

Macapá

Legend

Amazon Basin

Amazon River

River

Amazon River

BRAZIL

BOLIVIA

La Paz

Brasilia ★

Dusk in the Rain Forest

The Yagua Indian man crept through the Amazon rain forest in Peru. He had been hunting a family of red howler monkeys for hours. If he was successful, his family would eat meat that day. If not, they would go hungry. But it was nearly nightfall. He could not hunt much longer. Jaguars, snakes, and other dangerous animals came out to do their own hunting at night.

The howler monkeys stayed hidden behind a thick canopy of leaves. The Indian shifted from one foot to the other and lowered his blowgun. For an instant, a monkey showed itself, giving the Indian a perfect shot with his poison dart. Blowing a big puff of air through the pipe, he set his dart sailing. The poison dart hit its mark, striking a large female. The monkey gave a piercing cry and fell to the rain forest floor. She was dead.

Howler monkey in the Amazon rain forest.

The Indian ran to his quarry, picked up the monkey, and found an infant still clinging to his dead mother's back. He grabbed the monkeys and ran back to his village before darkness set in. The baby monkey sat, forgotten, in a villager's hut, cold and terrified. Left alone overnight, he grew weaker and weaker.

Yagua Indian with poison blowgun used for hunting.

A few miles down the Amazon River the next morning, ten-year-old Doyli woke up in her grass hut. She and her family lived on an island in the Amazon. This morning, she stretched and looked out her window. Many pairs of monkey eyes stared back. Now that the monkeys knew she was awake, they began chattering noisily. Doyli put on a T-shirt and shorts and went outside.

Baby monkeys were everywhere: red howlers, tiny marmosets that fit into the palm of her hand, woolly monkeys, a red uakari, monk sakis, and others. All were endangered species, and all were orphans rescued by Doyli and her Uncle Gilberto.

Without Doyli and her family, the monkeys would have died or lived miserable lives in captivity. But here, they were safe. Doyli petted and played with them. They made her happy, too. She laughed as a woolly monkey named Andres tumbled about the yard.

Pygmy marmoset

Red uakari

6

"There's more to caring for baby monkeys than playtime," she said, patting a furry head. She picked up a broom and swept the dirt yard clear of ant hills that had formed in the night. If she didn't brush away the tiny mounds, ants would swarm and bite the baby monkeys all day long.

As Doyli swept, she spied a dugout canoe paddling toward shore. Steering the canoe was the Yagua Indian hunter from the night before. Doyli ran down to meet him just as his canoe scraped ashore. Without saying a word, he handed her a limp, red howler baby. She took the monkey, nodded thanks to the Indian, and watched him paddle away.

Doyli lives in the Amazon in a house on stilts. Her front yard is under water for many months when the river rises.

Her best friend, a parrot named Aurora, sings duets with Doyli while she goes about her morning chores.

7

These forest Indians knew Doyli and her family took in orphaned monkeys and nursed them back to health. As soon as the little orphan was old enough to take care of himself, the hunter knew that Doyli and her family would set him free.

Doyli looked into the monkey's small, furry face. He was cold and dehydrated. It didn't look like anyone had fed him during the night. Without liquids, he wouldn't live much longer.

Doyli hurried him back to her hut and mixed a special formula. The foundling could barely swallow, but Doyli managed to get a little liquid into his stomach.

"Poor thing. Lost your mother, huh?" Doyli whispered. "I'll take care of you. See all of these monkeys? They were just like you once — scared and alone. But they're all right now. You will be, too."

Red howler monkey orphan.

She wiped away the formula that had trickled down the monkey's neck. She carried him to Uncle Gilberto.

"A Yagua man just brought him," said Doyli, handing the red howler to him.

"You've fed him?" asked Uncle Gilberto. He examined the baby howler for injuries. The little monkey appeared sound. Doyli nodded and stroked the reddish brown fur with a finger. She hated to part with him, but she had work to do.

"I have to get water for the rest of the monkeys," she said.

"I'll take him," said Uncle Gilberto.

9

Morning is the Time for Chores

Doyli picked up a bucket sitting on a wooden ledge on the porch. She carried it down a long, wooden staircase that led to the Amazon River. She scooped water into the bucket. Then, in one deft move, she balanced the full bucket on top of her head and carried it back to her hut. Her family would use the water for cooking, cleaning and drinking all day long. The monkeys and other animals would drink it, too. There was no running water inside her hut. They didn't have electricity either.

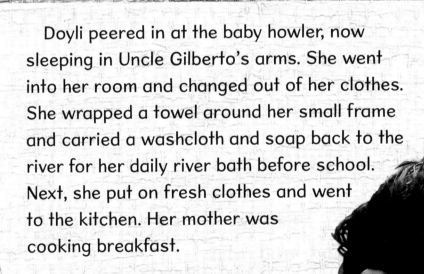

Doyli peered in at the baby howler, now sleeping in Uncle Gilberto's arms. She went into her room and changed out of her clothes. She wrapped a towel around her small frame and carried a washcloth and soap back to the river for her daily river bath before school. Next, she put on fresh clothes and went to the kitchen. Her mother was cooking breakfast.

"Hola, Mama," said Doyli.

"Good morning. Sleep well?" her mother asked, cracking an egg in the hot pan over the cooking fire. Doyli nodded and put her backpack on the floor next to the table. Her mother set a red plastic basin on the floor for the monkeys' food. Doyli mixed water and powdered milk. She swirled it around and around with a metal cup. Then, she ladled portions into smaller bowls and set them around the yard and porch. The monkeys lapped the milk.

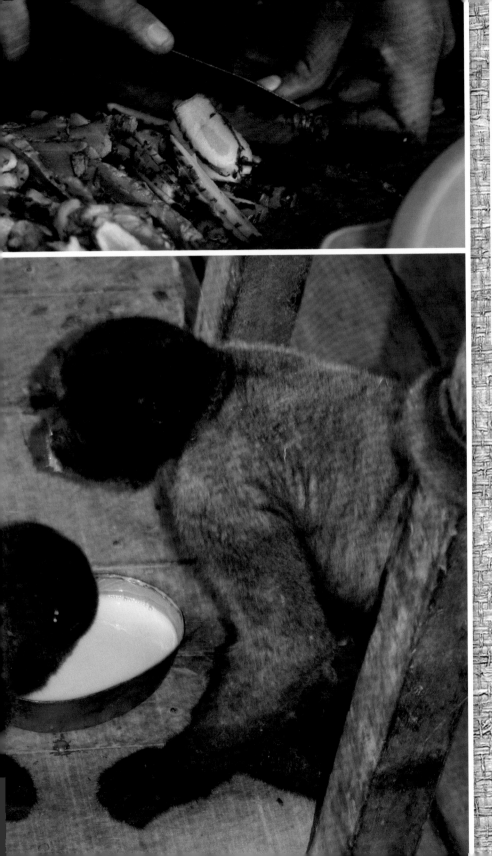

Milk wasn't all the monkeys had for breakfast. Doyli set out plates of chopped fruits and vegetables. The fruits were picked from trees her Uncle Gilberto had planted for the monkeys. Then Doyli sat down and ate her own breakfast of an egg, fried bananas, and milk — the same powdered milk her monkeys drank!

Now it was time for school. Doyli's mother and the monkeys followed her to the Amazon's shore to see her off.

13

The Journey to School

Doyli's older brother, Omar, rowed her across the Amazon in the family's dugout canoe. They passed a barge carrying enormous logs. The sight made Doyli angry.

"Why don't they stop cutting down so many trees?" she asked.

Her brother shook his head, but only said, "Greedy."

Doyli knew what he meant. He was talking about the greedy business of men and women cutting down big trees in the rain forest. To them, the logs were worth a fortune, but the trees were the monkeys' only home. Without them, where would monkeys live? Doyli feared that the monkeys would disappear forever.

The barge was headed for Iquitos, the nearest city, where the trees would be cut into boards for building houses. Doyli and her Uncle Gilberto traveled to the markets in Iquitos once a month to buy supplies. She had often seen the logs piled high on the side of the riverbank. She couldn't help but think of all the monkeys who had once called those trees home.

Suddenly, logs from the barge tumbled into the river! The great splash sent the little canoe careening. Omar tried to paddle quickly away from the enormous logs, which could easily smash their canoe into tiny pieces.

"Hold on!" he cried.

Doyli clung to the sides of the canoe as it was pitched from side to side. She didn't want to be thrown into the swift current, where flesh-eating piranha lurked. The logs created waves that drove their little canoe far off course, but Doyli and her brother managed to stay inside.

Piranha

The men working on the barge yelled to each other, scrambling to fish the logs out of the water. But they did not call out to Doyli or her brother to check on their safety. Omar was finally able to bring the canoe to shore, but Doyli was farther away from school than she usually was.

Sloth

"This makes a longer walk for you. Those barges are dangerous for the rain forest and for us!" he said.

"That's all right. I still have plenty of time. I'll just explain to the teacher what happened. Whew, that was scary," said Doyli.

She watched her brother turn the canoe back toward home. She hiked along the shore and found her familiar path through the jungle. Doyli passed land charred black, with smoke still rising from it — another section of rain forest had been burned for farming.

Doyli scanned the ground for baby sloths or monkeys that may have been abandoned in the chaos of the burn. Luckily, she saw none.

Doyli arrived at a second canoe lashed to a tree beside a lagoon. Enormous lily pads floated in the water. She looked into the water for caimans — crocodile-like animals — lurking in the water, but she didn't see any. They could be trouble! A large caiman could snatch a girl off the river bank and drag her into the water.

Doyli carefully paddled the canoe around the lily pads to the other side of the lagoon. Then she inched her way across a fallen tree. One slip, and she'd be ankle deep in mud.

Caiman

Doyli finally arrived at school after an hour. It usually took her forty-five minutes, but the scare on the river had made her journey that much longer. She tried to concentrate on her math, Spanish, and science lessons, but her mind kept wandering to the little monkey she'd cradled that morning. Would he still be alive when she got home? During recess, Doyli played soccer, but all the while she thought of the baby howler and wished she was home.

A girl rings the school bell. School is about to begin.

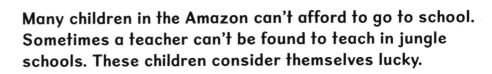

Many children in the Amazon can't afford to go to school. Sometimes a teacher can't be found to teach in jungle schools. These children consider themselves lucky.

Time for the Monkeys

After school, Doyli followed the same path home. She was anxious about the baby howler monkey. She needed to see whether he was still alive. When she arrived home, she pushed open her hut's door and threw her backpack on the table. She half expected to find Uncle Gilberto at his desk, the furry bundle gone. But, no! There he was snuggled on Uncle Gilberto's lap.

"He looks better," said Doyli.

"He just might make it. Infection can still set in when they're this weak and they don't have their mother's milk. Would you please take him?" asked Uncle Gilberto.

They shifted the bundle from the crook of his arm to Doyli's. She took the baby bottle from the desk and sat in a rocker, feeding the little howler.

Doyli whispers and sings, cuddles and kisses. She gives the little howler her strong medicine of love and nourishing food.

Just then, a juvenile howler monkey slipped in through a crack in the roof. Doyli called out to her uncle.

"Uncle Gilberto! The howler's inside!" cried Doyli. Her uncle hurried to the porch. He shooed the mischievous monkey down from the ceiling and back out the door, but not before he'd managed to pull out handfuls of the ceiling's grass thatch and throw them to the floor.

Naughty monkey!

"Ah, we'll get that later," said Uncle Gilberto, frustrated. The monkeys were cute, but they were mischievous. He checked Andres, a woolly monkey with a skin condition. Patches of his hair were falling out because of the island's sandy soil. Monkeys spend most of their time in trees in the wild, but here, Andres lived on the ground with his human family.

"Tomorrow is Saturday," said Uncle Gilberto. "We'll go to market in Iquitos. We need supplies."

Doyli smiled. She loved seeing the crowds of people and tables piled high with goods for sale. That night, she was so excited she had a hard time falling asleep.

The next day, Doyli and her uncle set off in their canoe before daylight. It would take four hours to get to the market. They passed the time looking at animals. A three-toed sloth slept in a branch overhanging the river. A tapir foraged at the river's edge. They even saw four pink river dolphins swimming near their canoe, popping their noses in and out of the water.

They saw other families on their way to the market, as well. Some had canoes laden with fruits to sell.

Tapir

At the market, Doyli wandered the crowded lanes. She saw flip flops in every color, jewelry made by Indians, and candy — so many good things.

The spicy scent of hot chilis wafted through the air, and the sounds of people shouting good-naturedly to one another, "Buy my rice. It is excellent quality!" could be heard. Doyli saw stalls with jars and bottles of homemade jungle medicine, mounds of sweet potatoes, and stalks of sugarcane.

Then Doyli's heart stopped for a moment. In a corner, she saw a baby spider monkey in a cage. It looked so frightened. Doyli knew that people sometimes tried to sell monkeys in the markets. And, she knew, too, that people sometimes bought them and turned them into pets. But the animals rarely lived. Monkeys need special diets that most human households can't provide. They belong in the wild, not trapped in small cages. The man selling the monkey saw Doyli.

"She's cute, isn't she? Would you like to buy her?" he asked.

Doyli shook her head, feeling sick. She crouched by the cage and put her fingers in to stroke the little monkey, but it shied away from her touch.

"Where is her mother?" Doyli asked.

"Oh, her mother died, I think. I found her in the forest. She was all alone and would have died, too, if I hadn't rescued her. Now she needs a home," he said.

Baby spider monkey

Monkey thief

26

Doyli didn't believe his story for one minute. She knew thieves killed the monkey parents to steal and sell the babies. She hurried away, looking for her uncle. She found him talking with some men. She ran up to him.

"Uncle Gilberto! I saw a baby spider monkey in a cage." Uncle Gilberto immediately turned away from the men, anxious to learn more about the captive monkey.

"Where?" he asked, leaning down. She pointed in the direction of the monkey thief.

"I'll take care of this," he said. He handed her some coins. "Buy yourself a soda pop. I won't be long."

Doyli bought a bottle of pop and positioned herself on a stool not far from the monkey seller. She waited and waited. Where had Uncle Gilberto gone? What was taking so long? What if someone bought the baby before her uncle returned? Doyli knew it was illegal to buy and sell monkeys, especially endangered ones, but people still did it.

She had finished her drink before Doyli saw Uncle Gilberto in the crowd. Two uniformed policemen trailed him. The man selling the monkey saw the policemen, too, and ran. One policeman ran after him. The other handed the monkey to Uncle Gilberto, who handed it to Doyli.

"Thank you, Officer. Letting those animals sit out in the hot sun without food or water is downright cruel," said Uncle Gilberto.

"I know you'll take good care of her," the policeman said to Doyli. She lifted the frightened monkey up and tucked the little one under her arm. Uncle Gilberto smashed the cage on the ground.

Doyli and Uncle Gilberto walked to their canoe already loaded with their supplies. They saw the policeman lead the monkey thief away. At least this man wouldn't be stealing any more endangered monkeys from the wild.

Home Again

Back home, Doyli fed the spider monkey. After a good meal, the infant revived quickly. The baby animal looked around her new home curiously. Doyli wondered if the little monkey knew that she was safe.

Doyli and her family sat down to a supper of rice and fried bananas. Uncle Gilberto told everyone how Doyli discovered the caged spider monkey. After dinner, Doyli did homework. Then she sat on her rocker, listening to the sounds of the jungle. The baby howler played on the floor. Doyli could see his stomach, round from all the milk he'd drunk that day. Two baby monk sakis lay curled on her lap. She felt the cool, dry pads of their fingertips on her skin.

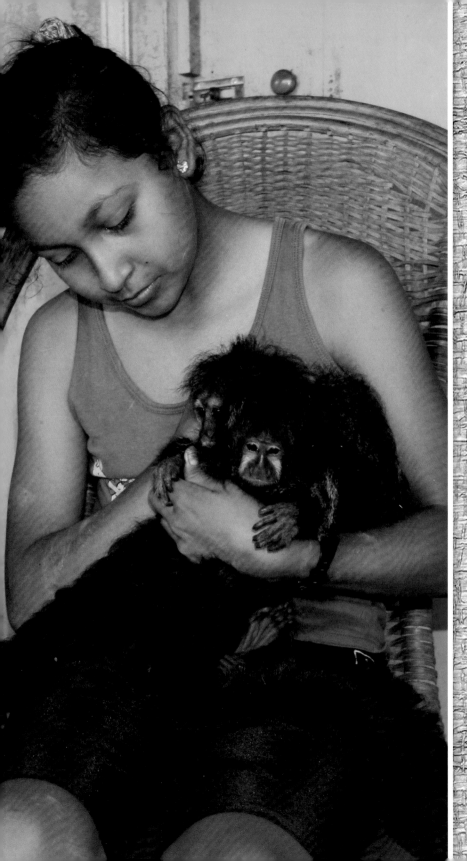

The moon sank below the trees. Doyli would have to get up and go to sleep soon. She looked out at the beautiful rain forest, aglow in the sunset. She knew she lived in an extraordinary land, with its unique wildlife and mighty river.

She slumped a little lower in her chair. The sun sank completely behind the trees. Uncle Gilberto set a lit candle on the table beside her. She smiled up into his kind eyes. She was grateful to be part of a family that cared so much for animals, saving lives that were so tiny — and so important.

"Good night, monkeys," she said. She gave the woolly monkey a good-night hug.

She lay down on her bed. Doyli drifted off to sleep to the sounds of crickets and frogs. She dreamt of the day when she would set all of her precious monkey babies free. They could live out their lives in the Amazon jungle, wild, as they were meant to live.

This woolly monkey came to the island as an orphan. Now she lives in the wild. But she brought her new baby back to meet Doyli.

To learn more about Doyli and other kids doing amazing things to protect wildlife around the globe, visit: WAKABooks.org.

What's Next?

A NOTE FROM THE AUTHOR

I am often asked how this story and book series came about. I'm also asked for follow-up ideas for kids and adults who want to learn more about projects by Doyli or others doing similar work around the globe.

Here's the story behind the story.

A few years ago, our family vacationed in the Amazon. We spent pre-dawn hours scanning the jungle for jaguars and monkeys and the rivers for pink dolphins. The Amazon is full of animals, but wild creatures are elusive. If you're lucky, you might catch a glimpse of a tapir slipping through foliage or hear the powerful blast of a howler monkey miles away.

As we slowly motored along a tributary, we passed an island on which a red uacari swung on a wooden railing. A pair of saddle-backed tamarinds chased each other over two tree stumps. A spider monkey sat in a small patch of grass in the dirt-swept yard of a stilted hut.

We asked our guide to stop there but he said, "Oh, no. That's a private home." He went on to say, "The family that lives there takes in orphaned and endangered monkeys on their own. They raise them and set them free again."

What? Our family *loves* animals. We begged until the guide agreed to contact the owners. "I'll ask," he said with a shrug.

Next day, miraculously, we were invited to visit. Stepping onto the island, we met a young girl with one saddle-backed tamarind on her head and one perched on her shoulder. My kids were in awe that this girl, Doyli, spent her days caring for such rare creatures. I thought other kids might be interested in her story, and the idea of a book came to me. We returned to Doyli's island several more times, documenting her life and her care of the monkeys.

I started thinking that there might be other kids around the world like Doyli: young people doing what they can to protect local wild animals.

It turns out there are. I've been privileged to be allowed to meet, interview, and photograph such kids going about their daily activities. Each child is fortunate to attend a school and has a loving family. And they do what they can, sometimes on their own, often with family and neighbors' support, to find a way to help wild animals thrive.

These stories shine a light on models of small-scale activism: young people who are kind, caring, and involved. We've all seen animals suffer, whether in person or via media. It's painful for us all. And we may think, "There's nothing I can do."

You *can* do something. You can get involved, too.

❖ ❖ ❖

This story is a seed. Maybe you and your friends and family can come up with something you can do, in a small way, to help protect other creatures who might need a helping hand.

For some ideas and stories of what others are doing around the world, visit www.WAKABooks.org.

WAKA stands for World Association of Kids and Animals. It's a way to share all these stories of kids – young people not so different from you and your friends – who found a way to get involved and help protect wild animals.

– Cathleen Burnham